Raised Without Worth, Crowned With Glory

by

Thuli Marutle Leigh

and

Anthony Oluwaseun Leigh

© 2025, Thuli Marutle Leigh
All rights reserved.

No part of this publication may be reproduced, distributed, or transmitted in any form or by any means, including photocopying, recording, or other electronic or mechanical methods, without the prior written permission of the author, except in the case of brief quotations used in reviews or articles.

This book is a work of nonfiction based on personal experiences and observations. Names and identifying details may have been changed to protect the privacy of individuals.

ISBN: 978-1-997482-04-8
Cover Design: Thuli Marutle Leigh
Author: Thuli Marutle Leigh
Co-author: Anthony Oluwaseun Leigh

Acknowledgment

This book was written from a place of remembering, healing, and reclaiming dignity. While it is inspired by real events and lived experiences, certain names, details, and events have been adapted, combined, or symbolically expressed to protect privacy and safeguard the integrity of all individuals mentioned.The purpose of this work is not to accuse, expose, or harm, but to give voice to a journey that many have lived in silence.

To my mother, Mrs. Bertha Marutle Ramahudu - you are the inspiration behind this book. Your strength, your grace, and your quiet endurance shaped every word on these pages. You taught us that even when the world overlooks you, your worth is not lost. It is waiting to be claimed. This story is a reflection of your courage and the legacy of resilience you gave to your daughters.

To my brother-in-law, Anthony Oluwaseun Leigh,thank you for walking alongside me through the writing of this book. Your guidance, insight, and support helped me give voice to memories that were heavy to hold alone. Thank you for honouring my truth with care and respect.

To my sisters - we rose.Not because we were welcomed,but because we refused to stay buried.

And to every woman who has ever been overlooked -may this story remind you that your worth was never theirs to give, and never theirs to take.

Table of Contents

Chapters:

1. WHEN JOY WORE MY NAME
2. THE GIRLS MULTIPLY — AND SO DOES THE BIAS
3. A QUIETLY BREAKING MARRIAGE
4. THE LAST NORMAL NIGHT
5. THE PINK TIE AND THE SIDE ROAD
6. AFTERMATH
7. A WIDOW, NOT A WEAKLING
8. THE DAUGHTERS THEY DISMISSED
9. GROWING UP AND BUILDING MY OWN LIFE
10. NAMES AND HOMES WE COULDN'T CLAIM
11. A MOTHER REBUILDS AND TEACHES ME STRENGTH
12. BOUNDARIES AND REACHING FOR PEACE
13. ERASED FROM MY OWN STORY
14. THE HOUSE THEY TOOK, THE FIGHT I DREAM OF
15. THE SONS THEY CHOSE — AND LOST
16. BREAKING THE SILENCE, OWNING MY STORY
17. CROWNED WITH GLORY
18. BUILDING A LIFE BEYOND THEIR EXPECTATIONS

'Out of the night that covers me, black as the pit from pole to pole, I thank whatever gods may be for my unconquerable soul. In the fell clutch of circumstance, I have not winced nor cried aloud.
Under the bludgeoning of chance, my head is bloody, but unbowed. Beyond this place of wrath and tears looms but the horror of the shade, and yet the menace of the years finds, shall find me unafraid. It matters not how strait the gate, how charged with punishments the scroll, I am the master of my fate: I am the captain of my soul.'
One Tree Hill Quote (3x06)

CHAPTER 1
WHEN JOY WORE MY NAME

The morning I was born was the day everyone had waited for. It was the morning when, finally, light shone on my family. Joy spilled into the streets of Sekhukhune. Sekhukhune is a district municipality in the southeast of Limpopo, at the northern tip of South Africa. It borders Mpumalanga to the east and Gauteng to the south. Sekhukhune has 117 wards and 764 villages. Neighbors still talk about my birth to this day. My mother went through the unimaginable—carrying me for ten months. In the end, she had a caesarean section just to bring me into the world.

My father, young, full of life, and giddy with his brown alluring skin color, smooth and sleek jaws in his aftershave, lifted his black boombox onto his shoulder and walked largely the dusty road outside our home, blasting Brenda Fassie's hit "Too Late for Mama" on repeat. The bass rattled the windows; the melody floated over corrugated roofs and mango trees. Children chased after him, barefoot, some on sandals, slippers, holed canvas, and with different shorts, loose shirts with slacked necks over saggy shoulders, and bare torsos beaming in ecstasy.

Women came to their doorsteps, wiping their hands on aprons to see what the noise was about, then followed with soft traditional dance hip-like movements. Men grinned and clapped him on the back, a thing of pride which sent a cold shiver of achievement down my dad's spine. He danced a little, smiling so wide you could see the gap in his teeth, shouting over the music that his first child had arrived, and of course, it didn't matter that I was a girl. That day, a firstborn was enough. That day, love was louder than idiosyncrasies in culture.

Inside, my mother froze multiple times as she cradled me, a tiny bundle with a name already chosen. They named me after my father's mother, a name woven with history and respect, a name deep in culture. My mother says she watched him outside, beaming with pride, and felt safe: whatever the future brought, she and her baby were wanted. For those first years, I knew only warmth and unfathomable love. The cry of a baby in the middle of the night was known to be a blessing, a promising future for the lineage of a family.

The house smelled of maize porridge in the morning and wood smoke from the coal stove in the evening. The floors were polished until they gleamed; the old radio hummed with gospel and kwaito when my mother cleaned. Laughter spilled from her as she bathed me, sang lullabies, and whispered prayers over my sleeping body. She was a housewife, but more than that — she was a quiet force, patient yet unshakable. Everything in my tiny world said: you are loved, you are enough, you are amazing, you are perfect.

My father's love showed up differently. He worked and provided; our bellies were full, our school shoes new, and our house felt secure. When he came home, he brought the smell of petrol and dust from long drives, the click of a briefcase, the thrill of coins for sweets. I didn't understand absence yet; I just knew that sometimes he was there and sometimes he wasn't, and when he was, everyone seemed lighter, everywhere beams brighter.

I remember his pride most of all. I love to fiddle with his clean-shaven and neatly curved chin any time he lifted me in his arms to play and chant my panegyrics. He'd scoop me up high and tell visitors, "This is my firstborn!" I remember the weight of his watch on my cheek when he hugged me, the shine of his shoes, the way he wanted me to stand tall. He wanted a bright daughter; I could feel it in the way he looked at me. He loved to hear me repeat his English phrases, smiling when I spoke clearly. He even bought me my very first book - Nelson Mandela's Long Walk to Freedom. I was far too young to understand every page, but to him it was a seed. He wanted me to know words, to own language, to have that distinguished and respected identity.

By the time I stepped into a classroom, English was already familiar to my tongue; my father had quietly built that foundation. If there were cracks, they were hairline and invisible to a child. Only later would I understand that joy can sit beside distance, that a father can adore you yet already be drifting away.

In those early years, though, I was safe. I was the celebrated firstborn, the little girl who made her father walk through town with music blaring and his heart wide open. I wish I could freeze that picture: my mother, young and glowing with purpose; my father proud and unguarded; our neighbors smiling as Brenda Fassie sang into the blue Limpopo sky. Before anyone whispered only girls, before my father's absences grew, before betrayal and grief and silence — there was this: a street alive with song because a daughter, a princess, had arrived.

When you flip the coin, I could do things that the boys can and couldn't do — male-dominated chores, like fire up my dad's engine while he was getting ready for work, and likewise wash it thoroughly and unbelievably clean. My dad was always impressed whenever I beat male gender to this extraordinary feat, and of course, my dad loved his toy so much, and for him to constantly compliment me meant I mastered the game.

He polishes his parabellum with great carefulness, without omitting any details of the hinges and corners. His work shoes are always a reflector that you could see your mirrored face enacting a caricature of your plain realities.

My best time is when he is about dressing for work. I perfectly knot his tie — you know, him being the superintendent of the traffic department — I love arranging his commendation pins.

CHAPTER 2
THE GIRLS MULTIPLY—AND SO DOES THE BIAS

By the time I was four, our house was no longer just mine alone—shared love without any blemish, a joy that wrapped us round. The surprise came one warm afternoon, an old white minibus, the kind that rattled and groaned up the dirt road, pulling to a stop outside our gate. The door slid open with a clank, and out stepped my mother, tired but smiling, a soft bundle wrapped in a blanket held close to her chest. My baby sister.

I remember running to the gate barefoot, giddy with joy, dust puffing under my feet, heart pounding with excitement. Neighbors peeked from doorways. Someone called out congratulations. In that moment, I was just a little girl thrilled to have someone smaller than me, a living doll to touch and help care for. The world still felt safe.

She was tiny and serious-faced, with a quiet watchfulness that made the grown-ups chuckle. I remember an older relative leaning over her crib, laughing, and saying, "Shame, the way she acts and looks, she could pass for a boy." As if being a girl was a flaw that needed excusing. Adults chuckled. My mother smiled politely, but I saw her shoulders stiffen.

And then, four years after that, came my second little sister—breathtakingly beautiful, with a softness that drew everyone's eyes. She was named after my paternal great-grandmother, while I carried the name of my paternal grandmother. Maybe it was superstition, maybe just the invisible threads of ancestry, but those names seemed to tie us to the same matriarchal line. From the start, we felt like soul twins, a mirrored strength running deeper than simple sisterhood.

Even as children, we were side by side; as teens, we shared secrets and rebellions; as grown women, we are still each other's first call, our bond stretching but never breaking.

Something shifted with each new sister. When I was born, the street had danced; my father had walked with a boombox, music shaking the dust. But with every girl after me, the celebration dulled—not garnished like the old theatre communal street performance expected, fewer choreographies to add color, less beautiful costumes dancing in unison, fewer songs in sonorous voices to paint the sky with love.

Relatives still came with gifts, though, but their words carried pity dressed as concern.
"Ah, don't worry, next time it will be a boy."
"She tried."

My father's family said it with the casual cruelty of people who think they're just stating facts. I felt the sting but tried not to show it. Instead, I wrapped a quiet shield around my sisters; they needed mental warmth more than I did. I told them stories about how beautiful and smart we were, how Daddy had once played music in the streets because of me, because a daughter was worth celebrating. I tried to block the stares, the whispers, the sighs… but how long could I hold back the tide? Children see more than adults realize.

Slowly, it started to make sense to them; the hidden started to become visible, it started to creep in, slowly, until it was obvious. My sisters began to catch the looks for themselves, to hear the pity in the voices, and started seeing the real and true shadows behind people's images. My protection could only stretch so far.

My mother fought in her own gentle way. She scooped us close and said:

"You are enough. My girls are beautiful, clever, and strong. Let no brute soul tell you otherwise."

Her silence spoke volumes to us; her unsaid carried gravity in interpretations she need not tell us. She never once let shame reach her lips. Yet I watched her swallow pain after each visit, her smile trembling as another neighbor offered sympathy for her "misfortunes," calling us daughters. I saw how she fought to stay proud even as the world tried to chip away at her joy.

Family gatherings sharpened the difference. Uncles would ask my father, saddened, when he would finally have a boy. Some clapped him on the back with that half-joking, half-serious tone men use when they think they're teasing but really aren't. Sometimes my father laughed along; other times his face tightened, and a silence followed him around the house that night.

Although I was just a little girl with little or no knowledge, my life had sharpened in due time, and the questions started to root:
Why are girls treated like a mistake? Why aren't we enough?

I didn't speak them aloud, but they lived in me. They pushed me to be clever, helpful, almost boy-like at times, desperate to prove that my existence wasn't a disappointment.

And still, life went on.

Ten years after that, my third sister—our youngest—arrived. The fourth girl. To the world, she was just another daughter, another "achievement" not to be celebrated, another sigh for a family that "still hadn't managed a boy." But to us, she was a blessing wrapped in pink. My mother had just graduated, finally carving a way toward independence, and she landed her first hospital job right after giving birth. It felt as though this tiny baby brought heaven's favor with her.

By then, I was in high school, inseparable from my mother—part daughter, part confidant, best friend. She worried aloud:

"How will I work nights with a newborn? Who will help me?"

Our family had long since faded into absence; her own parents were gone, and though my father had sisters, none offered a hand. My father himself loved the baby; she looked so much like him—beautiful, hairy, petite—but he was never truly present.

I wanted my mother to succeed, to rise above the gossipers who pitied her for having girls, to excel over the idiosyncrasy of a relic called tradition, not to be proud to ride on.

So I told her, "Don't worry, Mama. I'll take care of my baby sister."

She hesitated—
"But you have to go to school in the morning."

I said I knew, but we would make it work until she could afford help.

So, we did.

Each night my mother left for her hospital shift, and I stayed behind with the baby. I fed her, rocked her, studied with one ear open to every sound. I barely slept, but I didn't complain. I was determined to hold the fort for my mother until her first paycheck came and she could hire a nanny.

It was my first taste of adult responsibility, and of how women quietly hold each other up when the world looks away.

It was also around this time that the first real cracks in my parents' marriage stopped being whispers and turned into things I could no longer ignore...

CHAPTER 3
A QUIETLY BREAKING MARRIAGE

The first night I truly understood that my parents' marriage was cracking came while I was still half a child and half a stand-in mother. My baby sister lay asleep beside me, a tiny bundle who smelled of milk and warm blankets. I had promised my mom I would look after her while she worked the night shift at the hospital — her first real job after years of staying home, her first step toward independence.

I was in high school, exhausted but determined; I wanted my mother to succeed, to prove every gossip wrong, to shame every heart that staunchly believed in that barbaric idiosyncrasy of irrelevance of a girl child. It was quiet except for the faint hum of insects outside and the soft creak of our house settling.

Then I heard the front door open. Footsteps. Two sets.

I froze.

My father's voice floated down the hallway, low and casual — the tone he used when showing someone around:

"This is my aunt's room… this is my sister's room…"

He was giving a tour — but to whom?

My chest went cold.

And then I realized: he had brought a woman home.

A stranger's lighter laugh echoed behind him. My stomach knotted. My mother was away, working her first long night for a job that might finally give her freedom, and he was here with someone else.

The baby stirred, then started to cry — the thin, urgent wail of a newborn. I reached to soothe her, terrified to wake the whole house. Within seconds, my father rushed in, anger sharp in his whisper:

"I do not want to hear that baby crying."

I remember staring at him, shocked. How was I supposed to silence a week-old infant? Only later did I understand — he didn't want the woman to know there was a new baby in the house. My presence, my sisters, the proof of his family, were inconveniences to his performance of bachelor freedom.

He disappeared back down the hall.
The baby eventually quieted in my arms.
I sat awake the rest of the night, my heart pounding, rocking her gently while the man who was supposed to protect us walked another woman through the home my mother had just fought to keep afloat.

Life and its cruelty, I must say.

By the time my mother returned at dawn, I was bleary but smiling. I didn't tell her everything — not that night. She was already pushing herself beyond exhaustion: a brand-new baby, a new job, a husband who was supposed to help but drifted further away every day. I just handed her the sleeping child and said we were okay. I wanted to hold her up, just as she was trying to hold all of us.

It wasn't the first time she had felt abandoned. For years, whenever she dared complain that my father was never home, that he was stepping out of his marriage vows, his own family shut her down. One day, after she went to them desperate and humiliated, one of his sisters cut her with words she would never forget — words I heard with my own ears even though my mother had tried so hard to shield me:

"Leboga lesaka la bupi."

Be thankful for the sack of pap.
In other words: at least he buys you food, so stop expecting more.

They thought I was just a child and wouldn't understand, but I did. I held those words, heavy and unforgettable. My mother tried to hide the disrespect from me, but she couldn't control what people said in front of us. Those words settled inside me like a stone. That sentence burned something into my mother, too. If even his family thought she should be grateful for crumbs, then she would make sure she could stand without them.

My father could come and go as he pleased, but she quietly forced him to pay her university fees. No matter how much resistance, no matter how humiliated she felt, she made sure that education happened, come hell or high water. I think that was the moment she began to plan her survival: not loud, not dramatic, but determined. If this marriage would not honor her, she would at least build a future for herself and her daughters.

After that night, the pattern became clearer, not in explosions, but in quiet, wounding ways. My father was home less and less. When he did appear, he was distracted, sometimes charming, sometimes cold. The house filled with whispers that floated in on the wind: gossip from neighbors, cousins, family friends. I began to hear rumors that somewhere out there were other children — and some of them were boys. The very sons everyone pitied my mother for not giving him. People said their names in hushed tones, claiming to know the women.

My mother must have heard the same things; the township grapevine is hard to avoid, but she had changed by then. She didn't chase the whispers. She didn't beg. She didn't storm out looking for proof. She was too busy surviving. She was working long nights at the hospital, coming home exhausted to feed a baby and raise three older girls. She chose focus over scandal — as long as she didn't catch him red-handed, she refused to let rumors derail her. I think it was her way of protecting her sanity and her future.

She had already decided: if the marriage was breaking, she would not let it break her.
She would study, she would work, she would raise her daughters to stand tall even in a world that whispered they were not enough.

For me, it was more complicated. I still loved my father; he was mine. But each rumor, each whisper — there's another one, and it's a boy — chipped away at something inside me. I felt loyalty clash with hurt. I wanted him to choose us, to fight for us, to say that girls were enough — but the world kept rewarding him for leaving. The family that once celebrated my birth now acted as if it had finally redeemed itself elsewhere by fathering sons.

My mother rarely spoke of the betrayals out loud, but the silence in our house grew heavy. She kept moving, pushing, working, planning, holding us together. Her quiet strength became my blueprint: if no one will fight for you, you fight for yourself.

After that night and the whispers that followed, something hardened in me. I was still just a teenager, but I had already seen too much. My father's love had once felt proud and safe — now it felt conditional, drifting wherever his desire led him.

I remember lying awake after hearing yet another rumor about a son somewhere else, and thinking: How can a father's pride treat another woman's daughter like this? What if someday it were me? What if some man loved me only until something newer or easier came along? Would my father be proud if another man humiliated me the way he was humiliating my mother?

I made a private vow then — the kind a girl whispers into the dark:

I will never tie my life to a man who treats women this way.
I will never accept crumbs.
I will choose respect, or I will choose myself.

It was a quiet, fierce promise born from pain.
My mother had shown me how to endure, how to rebuild.
But I also wanted something more: a love that did not disappear,
a man who did not use daughters as bargaining chips
in a culture obsessed with sons.

Those nights watching my mother return from work
exhausted yet dignified,
those whispered rumors of half-brothers somewhere out there —
they became my compass.

They taught me what I would not settle for,
what I would demand from life.

CHAPTER 4
THE LAST NORMAL NIGHT

Some nights seem ordinary until memory burns them into something sacred. The evening before my father's accident was one of those nights. I cooked him one of his favorites: pap with a rich beef-bones stew — not just bones, but tender meat and bits of fat he loved, mixed with diced potatoes, and a side of soft, buttery cabbage. The alluring and captivating smell filled the house. My father ate with a usual unending appetite and delight, asking for more and teasing that I was finally a woman now that I could cook like this. My mother and he laughed so much that night — real laughter, the kind that felt rare after so many years of quiet distance. Even I laughed, warmed by the feeling of family. Looking back, it felt almost like a farewell we didn't know we were giving, a departure unforeseen, a thorny goodbye.

The next morning, he woke early to prepare for a close friend's wedding where he would stand as one of the groomsmen. He had just bought a brand-new black suit with a pink tie for the occasion, a suit so new it didn't need ironing. He asked me to help with the rest of his clothes for the trip: trousers, shirts, T-shirts, socks.

That morning, he showed me a life skill I had never learned: how to press a perfect crease down a pair of men's trousers. He demonstrated on one pair, guiding my small hands, explaining how to hold the iron so the line stayed sharp. When he was satisfied, he smiled and told me to pack everything neatly for him while he went to work. "I'll come back later to fetch the bag," he said. I was so proud. This was my moment to show him that his firstborn could take care of him.

I escorted him out, carrying my baby sister in my arms — she was only a year and a month old. As we reached the car, she waved a chubby little hand and beamed at him. My father leaned over and kissed her before getting in and driving off. It's a picture seared into me: the happy wave, the easy kiss, the quiet contentment of an ordinary morning.

After he left, I laid the baby down and got to work, ironing every pair of trousers just as he had taught me, folding shirts and T-shirts, pairing socks, carefully packing it all into his bag. I wanted him to open it later and feel proud of me.

That night before, our family had been laughing and sharing a meal. That morning, everything seemed fine, even joyful. None of us knew those would be the last hours we'd ever spend with him as a husband and father before everything fractured.

CHAPTER 5
THE PINK THE SIDE ROAD

After school that day, the sun was hot on the pavement and the air full of chatter. I was standing with one of my closest high school friends, laughing about something small and ordinary, when a familiar car slid to a stop at the red traffic light just a few meters away. It was my father. For a split second, warmth rushed in, the pride of seeing him out in the world, maybe on his way back to pick up the bag I had packed so carefully.

Then my eyes moved to the passenger seat.
A woman sat there.
Not my mother.

She was pretty, well-dressed, and comfortable enough to be laughing with him as if she belonged. The world seemed so still for a moment. My smile faltered. Heat rose up my neck — a rush of confusion, anger, pain, and shame. He looked straight at me. Our eyes met. He knew I had seen. The light turned green. Instead of turning toward home for the bag I'd packed, he drove on.

I knew then he wouldn't be coming back that afternoon.

I went home with a heart pounding too loud for my small chest. My mother was the first person I went to; she had always been my safe place. I told her what I had seen. She listened quietly, face still, taking in each word. She didn't cry in front of me; she never did. But I knew her too well. I could always tell when she had been crying: the slight redness around her eyes, the careful way she moved, the heavy silence that followed.

That night, the air itself felt swollen with unspoken pain.
It wasn't the first time she had been betrayed, not the first, but this was different. This time, her firstborn had become the witness. The betrayal had reached our doorstep through my eyes. Though she stayed composed, I could feel her heartbreak reverberate through the house. I have often thought that heaven itself must have heard her silent grief that night, because as my mother wept quietly out of sight, somewhere out on the road, my father's car sped toward the wedding he was supposed to attend.

He never came back.

Late that evening, as thick silence still hovered on our roof, the phone rang — sharp, urgent. There had been an accident.
My father was in the hospital.

Something inside me went still. I didn't cry; I felt hollow.
I think a part of me already knew. The night before, the betrayal, my mother's pain — it was as if some unseen thread had already snapped.

Then the whispers turned to truth: he hadn't been alone.
The woman who had been laughing in the passenger seat survived the crash, but she lost a leg and would spend the rest of her life in a wheelchair. That knowledge hit like another collision: not just losing my father, but knowing that his final moments were spent beside someone who wasn't my mother, someone whose presence had already broken her heart. It was a humiliation laid over grief, a betrayal carved into the story of his death.

When the final call came, that he hadn't survived, the hollowness deepened. My mother's scream split the air; the kind of sound that doesn't just echo, it lives in the walls. She had loved him since high school, given her youth, her trust, her whole heart. Now, in one phone call, it was over and the whole village would know he died with another woman by his side.

I stayed frozen, angry and numb at once.
Angry that he had chosen someone else over coming home that day.
Angry that he had risked everything for a fleeting thrill.
Angry because maybe, just maybe, if he had come home first and faced what I'd seen, none of this would have happened.

Then came the most haunting detail of them all — the black suit and the soft pink tie, the ones he had bought with pride to stand beside his friend as a groomsman, never made it to the wedding. They became the clothes we buried him in.

I remembered how he had held that tie up just days before, playful and pleased, asking if it matched the shirt. He had chosen it to celebrate life and friendship; instead, it became the ribbon of his own farewell. When I saw him lying in the coffin, still and unreachable, wearing that brand-new suit and the gentle pink tie, something inside me shattered. Everything in me died without hope of awakening again.

I hadn't cried until that moment.
But seeing him dressed in joy and lowered in sorrow broke me.

Childhood ended there — with a tie meant for celebration turning into a symbol of loss and betrayal. Reality patted me on my back and whispered:

"The tide of life flows unspoken and moves in discreet; everyone is either a victim or a victor, notwithstanding."

Then a subtle voice, very subtle and crystal clear like a distinct water's echo, said:

"No one is immortal or immune to death. Karma never sleeps, so is Hades. Everyone will be paid back awfully in their coins if they decide to neglect the essence of life and turn their backs on vows they once made and commitment to."

CHAPTER 6
AFTERMATH

The house felt wrong after the accident — not just quiet, but hollowed out. Smiles vanished without being told, and sadness hovered above the roof, forming black clouds. People came and went in waves: neighbors bringing food, relatives arriving with heavy faces, whispers filling the air. Everyone seemed to know what to say to each other, except to us. And beneath every whisper was the detail none of us could escape: he had not been alone.

The woman who had sat laughing in the passenger seat survived the crash. She would live, but with one leg gone and a wheelchair in her future. The knowledge hung over our mourning like a second funeral: we were burying a husband and father while the woman he betrayed, my mother, was left another victim, life played a fast one on.

The confrontations my mother lived on, a permanent reminder of the wound. It wasn't gossip; it was fact, and it added humiliation to grief. People didn't know whether to pity us or judge us, so they did both in hushed voices just loud enough to reach our ears. In our culture, grief is often dressed up as strength. During that first week, we were told again and again:
"Don't cry. Be strong. What will people say if you break down?"

My sisters and I were young, but we understood the command: stay composed, do not show the depth of your hurt. Even my mother, raw with heartbreak and betrayed twice over, was urged to hold her tears back. It was as if our loss had to be tidy for everyone else's comfort. I stayed mostly silent, but my body buzzed with unspoken anger and confusion. My father had left for a celebration and never returned; now we were expected to perform dignity instead of grief. And beneath it all, I was furious: he hadn't just left us; he'd been on his way to joy with someone else when everything ended.

There were crowds at the funeral — colleagues, friends, neighbors, family. Many of them promised loudly:
"Don't worry, we are here for you. We will stand by you."

They said it with easy warmth, as though the future would be gentle. At the time, I wanted to believe them, but something in me kept my hopes at bay, fingering my naivety, thereby jolting my reality.

My father's family arrived in numbers, proud and loud. But beneath the hugs and handshakes, there was an invisible line, an unspoken sense that we were only daughters and that somehow that lessened our place in this legacy. Even in mourning, I felt it: the old bias creeping back through the cracks of our grief. It was subtle but cold — a certain way they addressed my mother, a certain way they avoided meeting our eyes too long, the quiet celebration of the sons who were elsewhere, and the short stare after, then quickly looking away after our eyes met from a distance.

Some whispered about the other woman, half blaming my mother, half excusing him as if betrayal and death could coexist without consequence for his legacy. When the coffin was lowered, my tears finally came, hot and unstoppable. The pink tie glinted softly in the sunlight one last time before the lid closed. All I could think was how fast love turns to loss, how fast a family can be left to fend for itself — and how deep a father's choices can cut when they echo in death.

In the days that followed, the promises began to fade almost immediately. The phone calls slowed; the visitors thinned out. People who had said,

"We're your family, we'll be here,"

disappeared back into their own lives.

My father's friends stopped checking in. His relatives, the same ones who had spoken so loudly about support, seemed to move on without us. Not long after the funeral, my mother and I went into town to buy a few things. Life had to go on somehow, even if our hearts were still raw; life indeed was a poor player.

As we stood in line at the supermarket, I looked up, and there she was — the woman from the passenger seat. She was the cashier now, seated in a wheelchair, her face older than I remembered, one leg gone. The sight stole my breath for a moment. Here was the living reminder of that night: the woman who had laughed beside my father while my mother cried at home, now permanently marked by the crash they never came back from.

I didn't feel triumph, only a heavy, complicated sorrow. She had not been the only one to blame; my father had made his choices too — perhaps more than she had. Yet here we all were: my mother and I, shopping to rebuild a life that had been ripped open; she, trapped in a chair for life, paying a price no one could have imagined.

It was a silent confrontation — no words exchanged, just eyes meeting for a brief, raw second, but it said everything about betrayal and consequence.

My mother was left with four girls and a pile of unfinished dreams. She had no parents to lean on. My maternal grandparents were long gone, and no sisters to hold her up. The sisters my father had had, the ones she once hoped would stand beside her, began to drift away, too. Some of them barely acknowledged her, as if widowhood and betrayal had turned her invisible.

I remember watching all of this with a sharp, growing awareness. The injustice was clear, even to me as a teenager. We had just buried the man who was husband, father, provider — and yet his death seemed to strip us not only of him, but of the respect and belonging we had once been promised.

It was during those days that I began to understand how fragile security can be for women and children in a world that measures worth by the presence of sons, and how a man's choice can leave his family unprotected in life and humiliated in death. The same people who had laughed with us when my father was alive now treated my mother like an afterthought.

I could see it hurting her, but she straightened her back, dried her hidden tears, and began to plan.

CHAPTER 7
A WIDOW, NOT A WEAKLING

After the funeral, the house felt emptier than ever — but my mother refused to let emptiness define us. For a short while, she moved through the fog of grief, quiet and deliberate, but soon a new kind of fire lit in her. The same woman who had been told to "be grateful for a bag of pap," the same wife who had spent years patching up a love full of holes, decided she would not stay powerless.

People expected her to crumble. Many assumed she would spend the rest of her life waiting for help from my father's family, but my mother had been preparing long before tragedy struck. She had studied while raising children. She had gone back to work even when her youngest was just days old — taking night shifts before her body had healed because she knew she would one day need her own way out. Exhaustion was the price she was willing to pay for security. Now, with him gone, that preparation became her lifeline.

The city house, once a sign of our family's stability, became something darker: a place where my father's relatives came and went as if it belonged to them. They treated my mother like a guest in her own home. They walked in without asking. They made decisions without consulting her. Not one of them asked:

"How are you holding up? Do you need anything? How are the children?"

There was no emotional support, no practical help, no concern, no console — just entitlement. My mother quietly reached her limit. One day, she decided she would not live at the mercy of people who had never cared about her well-being. She sold the house. To outsiders, it seemed shocking — even rebellious. The whispers began: How dare she sell his house? But that decision was not rebellion. It was survival. It was dignity.

It was a widow saying, "You will not invade my life and call it help. You will not control me through bricks and walls that you think you own." She took the money, bought a new house in her own name, and built a space no one could claim, no one could enter without respect. It was hers, ours, safe.

That home became the physical proof that even without a man, a woman can choose freedom. Life without my father wasn't easy. As teenagers, we sometimes lost our way, the kind of stumbles that come with grief and growing up.

We made mistakes, tested boundaries, and tried to navigate a world without his presence. Whenever word of those missteps reached my father's family, they were quick to judge. They blamed my mother for our every imperfection, forgetting that they were parents too and that teenagers everywhere sometimes drift, especially after losing a father. None of those critics had stepped in to help us heal, yet they were quick to condemn.

But my mother never gave up on us. She stayed present, disciplined with love, patient but firm. She put us back on a straight and narrow path, not through fear, but through quiet consistency and resilience. Slowly, we steadied ourselves, learned from our mistakes, and found our footing again. She did that alone, with no one to lean on but herself.

Her determination became our silent inheritance. She didn't sit us down to say, "Girls, you are strong," she showed us. She showed us that a woman abandoned and underestimated can still rise, study, work, build a home, and raise daughters who stand tall. The same pain that had silenced her when my father was alive became the fuel that rebuilt our lives after he was gone.
The day she sold that house and bought another was more than a property deal. It was a declaration:

> "You may have stripped me of support, but you will not strip me of power."

Looking back now as a woman and a mother, I realize that this was the moment my definition of strength was born. Strength wasn't loud or showy — it was my mother's quiet defiance, her refusal to crumble when left alone with four daughters and no safety net. Watching her taught me that even when the world dismisses you, you can rebuild, protect your children, and claim a life on your own terms. Her fight became the blueprint for mine.

CHAPTER 8
THE DAUGHTERS THEY DISMISSED

We grew up in the shadow of whispers that said we were not enough. For years, the story of our family, at least the version told by my father's side, was that my mother had failed by having only girls. They pitied her, they pitied us. We were treated as though our existence was an unfinished sentence waiting for a son to complete it. But slowly, quietly, my sisters and I began to rewrite that story. It didn't happen overnight. Life after my father's death was hard. We had lost our anchor, and though our mother was strong, grief is a heavy fog for teenagers to navigate. We stumbled, made mistakes, and sometimes lost our way. When word of our stumbles reached my father's family, they were quick to judge and blame my mother:

"Look, they're going astray because there's no man in the house."

Not one of them stepped in to guide or support us, but they were loud in their condemnation. My mother didn't let it break her. She stayed present, disciplined with love, patient but firm. She kept pulling us back to center until, slowly, we steadied ourselves and found our way again. Then we began to rise. We studied. We worked. We built lives for ourselves piece by piece. My sisters each found their own paths — careers, education, families — and I built mine too, leaning on the fire my mother had passed down. Over time, the "girls who weren't enough" became accomplished, independent women. And something strange happened: the very people who had pitied or ignored us began to show interest again. It started with small things, a congratulatory text here, a call out of nowhere:

"I heard you finished your degree! That's wonderful."

"Your sister is doing so well at work, tell her we're proud."

An aunt who hadn't called in years suddenly phoned me and spent the first five minutes reminiscing about my father before asking about my job and where I was living. Another relative who had once spoken down to my mother sent me a message out of the blue:

"We're so proud of what you girls have become."

Invitations began to arrive — weddings, parties, family events we had never been included in before. It was as if success had finally earned us an invitation to our own bloodline. But none of it came with the one thing that mattered most: acknowledgment of my mother.

They praised us but never said, "We're sorry for how we treated her."

They wanted to know her daughters, but they still did not honor the woman who had raised us alone, with no help, no phone calls, no concern when we were hurting. I found myself caught between two longings:

• The longing for family, for peace, for some kind of connection to where I came from.

- And the fierce instinct to protect my mother, to refuse any relationship built on ignoring her pain.

I remember one phone call in particular, an uncle who had not spoken to us since my father's funeral rang me out of nowhere. His voice was warm, casual, as though we had always been close. He congratulated me on my work, asked about my children, then laughed and said, "You know, you girls turned out well after all."

I hung up politely but was unsettled. After all, as if we were a gamble that had finally paid off. Each message, each sudden compliment, felt both validating and hollow. Where were they when we were fatherless teenagers, grieving and drifting? Where were they when my mother was working nights and crying quietly behind closed doors? Now that we were successful, they wanted to claim us, but they had never claimed her. I decided early: if anyone wanted a relationship with me, it would have to begin with respect for my mother. You cannot love me and dismiss the woman who gave me life and sacrificed everything to raise me. Reconciliation, if it was ever going to happen, had to start with accountability.

My mother, though, never poisoned our hearts. She didn't tell us to hate them. She let us choose. She held her dignity quietly and continued her life. We learned from her calm strength: be polite, but know where you stand.

CHAPTER 9
GROWING UP AND BUILDING MY OWN LIFE

Adulthood arrived almost and crept in quietly, without the fanfare or guidance I once wished for. I left the small world of childhood, the house that had shifted and sighed under the weight of other people's judgments, and built a life with my own two hands. When I became a mother, it didn't feel foreign. Long before I held my first baby, life had already trained me. As a teenager, I had rocked my youngest sister through long nights so our mother could work. I had learned to change diapers half-asleep, to listen for a baby's breath in the dark, to keep the house steady while exhaustion pulled at me. Those years had been hard, but they had also taught me competence and quiet strength. So, when my own baby arrived and my mother, now a grandmother, asked gently, "Do you need help? This is your first child," I smiled and said, "Don't worry, Mom. I got this," I truly meant it. I realized then how much everything that happened to me — the pain, the responsibility, the early adult roles I carried — had shaped me into a woman who could nurture and stand strong.

I married young enough to still believe in possibility, old enough to know that love is a choice you work at. With my husband, I tried to create the home my mother had fought to give me: steady, safe, open with laughter. We built traditions from scratch, shared meals, silly dances in the kitchen, and the warmth of prayers whispered over sleeping children.

Holding my first baby girl cracked something open in me: a fierce tenderness and also an ache I didn't expect. I loved her beyond words, but I also felt the echo of all the pity that had hung over my own mother. I remembered the whispers: only girls, shame. I looked at my daughter's perfect face and swore she would never feel unwanted. I would teach her — early and often — that she was enough.

When I had another daughter, the old comments surfaced again, sometimes softly, sometimes with the casual cruelty of tradition. Neighbours, even distant relatives, would offer that half-smile, half-sympathy that had once broken my mother's heart. "Ah, two girls," someone said once, as though my family were an unfinished project. I held my head high and smiled anyway. But inside, a small sadness stirred: how long must this myth survive, that a woman's worth — and a child's value — are tied to a Y chromosome?

Years later, I gave birth to a son. The response was almost deafening in its difference. Calls, messages, and congratulations poured in. But threaded through the joy were words that stung: "You finally did what your mom couldn't."

"At last, a boy! Now your family is complete."

The world didn't know how those sentences landed. They were meant as praise, but each one pressed a thumb into an old bruise. My mother's love had been enough.

Our family — all girls — had been whole, and yet here they were, rewriting her story and mine: as though my son had somehow redeemed generations of women. I loved my boy deeply; he is joy, light, a miracle. But I refused to let his arrival erase my daughters or the women before him. I swore to myself that I would raise my son to do better, to honor and respect women, to know that girls are not less. I would teach him kindness, empathy, and strength without cruelty. I wanted him to grow up seeing his sisters and his mother as whole and worthy, and to carry that belief into every room he enters.

Becoming a mother also gave me new eyes for my own childhood. I saw my mom differently — the nights she stayed awake with babies and heartbreak, the quiet strength that carried us through. I began to understand her sacrifices not as ordinary but as extraordinary. And I carried her lessons: protect your children, stand tall even when the world doubts you, work hard to build dignity that no one can take.

Adulthood gave me love, family, and a voice — but it also showed me how deeply old wounds can hide inside celebration. Even as I built a new home, the echo of the past whispered: "girls are not enough." I fought it quietly, raising my daughters and son to know otherwise, even as the outside world tried to teach them the old song. It was in this season of building and protecting that other reckonings would come — reckonings about names, inheritance, and the unseen rules that still tried to decide who belonged.

CHAPTER 10
NAMES AND HOMES WE COULDT CLAIM

Names carry power. They tell the world who you belong to, what history you stand on, and where you come from. For boys in my father's family, that power was handed over without question. For me, it was always just out of reach. From the time I was little, my mother wished I had carried my father's surname. It wasn't that my father objected — he simply didn't make it a priority. He saw no urgency because I was a girl. "One day she will marry and change it anyway," was the quiet reasoning that floated around, unspoken but understood. As though my identity was temporary, waiting to be exchanged for my husband's. It didn't seem fair even then, but as a child, I couldn't fight it. My mother could only do so much; her hands were full with keeping a family afloat while living under a shadow of betrayal and silence. After my father died, I decided to try for myself.

I wanted, at the very least, to stand under my father's name — to reclaim that simple right for me and for my mother, the wife he'd married but whose place was so easily erased. I went to Home Affairs full of determination, carrying every paper and memory I could gather. The official was kind but firm: a relative from your father's side must come to confirm your place in the family. Without them, the process would stop. So, I began to call. I called aunts and uncles. I explained gently, respectfully, sometimes pleading. Each time there was an excuse — too busy, not nearby, another time. Sometimes there was silence. Sometimes there were promises that faded into nothing. Weeks became months, then years. The door remained closed.

And yet, for the sons my father had outside his marriage, the process was swift. Papers signed. Surnames granted. No endless phone calls. No cold refusals. Watching that unfold was a wound I carried quietly, not just disappointment, but confirmation of something deeper: in this family, a daughter's belonging was negotiable, a son was automatic. Property carried the same silent law.

We even had to struggle for something as simple as a key — the key to my father's own house in the village. The home where my mother had once been the wife and keeper and a home that everyone knew belonged to my father had somehow slipped from her hands. When she needed to enter after his death, we had to ask, explain, wait, and then finally, seek permission. My mother — a whole wife — stood outside and requested access to her own husband's home while the sons already had extra keys. That day etched itself into me: the quiet humiliation, the way dignity was chipped away not with violence but with small, deliberate exclusions.

My mother and I were denied entry to spaces that should have been ours by right, homes built and filled during her marriage. Doors that would not open for us swung wide for the sons. They moved freely, used what they needed, sometimes even lived in places my mother had once helped fill. We, meanwhile, were treated like outsiders asking for favors.

CHAPTER 11
A MOTHER REBUILTS AND TEACHES ME STRENGTH

Even before my father died, while betrayal and distance had already crept into our home, my mother was quietly rebuilding. Many expected her to shrink under disappointment, but she didn't. She was a young wife who had been pitied for giving birth only to daughters, humiliated by whispers, and left to raise us with little protection from the family that should have stood beside her. Yet, instead of folding, she began to build a future of her own. I watched her go back to school with babies underfoot. She sat for long hours at the kitchen table, textbooks open, notes spread beside baby bottles and dinner plates. Sometimes she studied late into the night, her eyes heavy but determined. She refused to let tragedy — or patriarchy — decide her story. When she graduated, the pride in our house was electric. For the first time in years, I saw her walk with shoulders straight and a quiet fire in her step.

Soon after, she got her first hospital job, just after giving birth to our youngest sister. While others might have seen only a burden, my mother saw hope: new work, new independence, new life. She stepped into that job not as someone waiting to be rescued but as a woman who had chosen to rise. Money was still tight, but she began to make choices that signaled freedom. One of the most powerful was selling the city house she had once shared with my father and buying her own home. It caused backlash; whispers flew about how dare she make such decisions without the family's blessing, but she held her ground. She chose a house that was hers alone, a place where her daughters could belong without asking permission, a space no one could take away. It wasn't just the house or the degree — it was the quiet message she gave us every day: "You do not have to stay small. You do not have to accept crumbs just because you are women. Build. Claim space. Own your life."

She also taught me something about peace — the hard, dignified kind. She didn't chase after every insult, didn't fight every unfair locked place on a door; she chose her battles carefully. "Some fights cost too much of your soul," she would say. "Sometimes winning isn't worth what you have to become." She wanted us to rise above pettiness, to keep our dignity even when wronged. Watching her rebuild changed me. It showed me that strength isn't always loud. Sometimes it's a woman studying at midnight after a day of work and heartbreak. Sometimes it's selling a house to buy freedom. Sometimes it's refusing to bow but also refusing to become bitter. Her life became a blueprint I would follow: "Keep your head high, work hard, educate yourself, create stability even when no one hands it to you." She didn't just raise daughters; she raised warriors cloaked in grace.

I didn't realize it then, but every time I watched her fight quietly for a future without losing her kindness, she was preparing me for my own battles. She was teaching me that dignity and resilience can outlast injustice. And soon, I would need those lessons because while my mother had already begun to stand on her own, the family that had shut us out was not finished with rewriting our story. The day would come when I'd try to reach for peace — and discover how costly the truth could be.

CHAPTER 12
BOUNDARIES AND REACHING FOR PEACE

By the time I was deep into adulthood, I had built a life of my own, a marriage, children, and work I loved. Yet a quiet hope stayed alive inside me: that one day, the children my father had scattered across different lives might find one another and build something healthier. We hadn't created the hurt; we were just born into it. The rivalries, the silence, the favoritism — those belonged to the adults. Surely, I thought, we didn't have to repeat them.

So, one day I decided to try. I asked around for contacts, slowly collecting phone numbers of the other children my father had fathered outside his marriage. Some relatives were reluctant, but I persisted. I thought if I, the first child of his marriage, reached out, maybe we could meet each other on neutral ground. No blame, no drama — just siblings finally acknowledging each other. When I had enough numbers, I created a WhatsApp group. I introduced myself simply:

"Hi everyone, I'm Pebetse. I started this group so we can get to know each other as siblings. I'm the first child of James, and he was married to my mother."

I wanted to set the tone: respectful, factual, and inclusive. I wanted my mother's place and, by extension, my own, to be known and respected. But almost immediately, the reaction was not what I hoped. Instead of welcome, I felt a wall slam shut. Some grew cold and distant. Others were openly hostile. Within hours, word had spread to the wider family, the very family that had once ignored us. Soon, I was receiving calls and messages, not of warmth, but of anger. One phone call burned into my memory. A relative's voice came sharp and accusing:

"Who do you think you are? You talk too much.

You're not even the firstborn — stop acting like you know everything!"

The words hit harder than I expected. My whole life, I had known myself as my father's first child. My father had raised me as his first. My mother had honored that place. Now, suddenly, I was being told to sit down, be quiet, and accept a different narrative — one that erased me to elevate someone else.

I remember sitting alone after that call, stunned, hurt, and full of questions:

"What had I done wrong? Was it a crime to say that my father was married to my mother? Was the marriage supposed to be a secret? Was I not supposed to introduce myself as the firstborn? Was I meant to protect everyone else's feelings at the cost of my own truth? I hadn't started the group to cause pain. I had hoped for a connection. But instead of curiosity or gratitude, I was met with anger, as if telling the truth about my parents' marriage was a personal attack."

Part of my desire to speak up came from years of watching my mother's place be dismissed. She had been the wife. The one who built a home, endured betrayal, stayed, and still raised us when he died. Why should her name and by extension my place as her first child be hidden? And beneath this wound was another, older one: the surname. My mother had always wanted my last name changed to my father's. It wasn't that my father refused; he simply didn't make it a priority. After all, I was a girl; someday I would marry and change it anyway. That was his quiet reasoning. But was that really enough? Was it fair that my identity be treated as temporary just because of my gender?

After his death, I pushed to make the change myself. I went to Home Affairs in South Africa, armed with hope, but they told me one of my father's relatives would have to be present to acknowledge me officially. I asked. I called. I pleaded. Each time there was an excuse — too busy, not available, some other reason. They never came. And yet, when it came to the sons my father had outside his marriage, there was no delay. Papers were signed. Names were changed. Doors opened easily for them.

It was a wound I carried quietly, a reminder that in this family, being a girl meant your belonging was always conditional, your identity always negotiable.

So, when I reached out that day, created that group, and introduced myself proudly as my father's firstborn, the daughter of his marriage, I wasn't just seeking connection. I was trying to reclaim the dignity long denied to my mother and to me. And instead of being met with understanding, I was punished for daring to speak. That moment hurt more deeply than I expected. It was a rejection not just of me, but of my history and of the truth my mother had lived.

But I chose not to let their reaction erase me. I didn't fight or beg for acceptance. I didn't rewrite my story to soothe their pride. I held my truth quietly and kept living, just like my mother had done all those years before. Their anger did not undo the love my parents had once shared, the marriage they had, or the life my mother built. It did not erase me.

And though it stung, it taught me something I would carry into the battles still ahead: my worth and my mother's honor could not depend on their approval. The family might try to rewrite our place, but the truth stood firm.

Next would come harder reckonings: homes, property, and the fight for dignity that my mother chose to meet with grace rather than conflict.

CHAPTER 13
ERASED FROM MY OWN STORY

After the WhatsApp group backlash, I told myself I would stay calm. I had reached out with respect and been met with anger; I thought perhaps the storm would pass if I stayed quiet. But it didn't. The storm grew. It wasn't enough for some relatives to be annoyed; they wanted to rewrite me.

Calls came, one after another, each more cutting than the last. Some were from people who had barely been present in my life, yet suddenly felt entitled to decide where I belonged. Their voices were sharp, urgent, almost panicked, as if the truth I had spoken threatened the story they wanted to keep.

"Stop saying you're the firstborn."

"You talk too much."

"You're disrespecting your elders."

"You have no right to speak about the marriage."

Each word landed like a slap. These were the same people who had disappeared when my father died, who had not helped us grieve, who had left my mother to raise four daughters alone. Now they were showing up only to erase me.

One conversation I will never forget: a woman whose approval had never been mine to seek called and shouted down the line, "You are not the firstborn! Stop lying. Stop acting like you know everything!"

I sat there stunned, phone pressed to my ear, my hands shaking. How could people who had abandoned us now rewrite the most basic truth of my life? My father had married my mother. I had been his first child within that marriage. My place was not a theory, it was a fact, practical. Yet here they were, trying to strip it away because it did not fit the story they preferred. It wasn't just about me. It was about my mother. To erase my place was to erase her marriage, to downgrade her from wife to something less. It was to say the years she spent building a home, bearing betrayal, and still standing tall were worth nothing. It was to undo her dignity in one sweep.

I remember putting the phone down after one of those calls and whispering into the empty room:

"What did I do wrong?"

"Was it a crime to say my father had been married to my mother? Was the marriage supposed to be a secret? Was I meant to hide and let another version of our story live, just to keep the peace? I hadn't started the group to shame anyone. I had only wanted connection, honesty, perhaps even healing. But telling the truth about who I was - who my mother was - had triggered rage."

For days, I carried a strange heaviness, part hurt and part disbelief. The rejection felt personal, but it was bigger than me. It was about gender and power, the same silent rule that had always favored sons and diminished daughters. The same mindset that had let them change their surnames easily while blocking me. The same one that had given them keys to houses while my mother asked for permission. Now it wanted to decide even my story, my birthright. Yet somewhere inside, another feeling stirred: defiance.

I would not erase myself to make others comfortable. I would not rewrite history to soothe pride built on our exclusion. My mother had taught me dignity, and part of dignity is refusing to disappear. I didn't argue with those who shouted. I didn't beg for their approval. I chose silence not because they were right but because I knew the truth didn't need their permission. I stayed rooted in what I knew: my mother's marriage was real, her love was real, my place as her first child was real. Their anger could not change that.

It hurt, yes, but it also clarified something: some doors would never open, no matter how gently I knocked. Some people would always choose a narrative that protects their own standing rather than acknowledge ours. And I had to decide: will I spend my life fighting to be seen by those determined to look away, or will I keep living, keep rising, keep telling the story as it happened?

I chose the latter. Being erased from my own story was painful, but it was also freeing. It forced me to stop waiting for certain people to validate me. It pushed me to own my truth fully, even if it meant standing alone. And from that place of quiet strength, I kept walking towards a future I would define myself, towards a voice I would no longer mute, and towards a life where my daughters, and even my son, would learn that no one has the right to rewrite who they are.

CHAPTER 14
THE HOUSE THEY TOOK AND THE FIGHT I DREAM OF

There are nights when my mind drifts to the house that should have been ours. Not just any house, the house in the village. The one my paternal grandparents once lived in. The one that has always been the center of family life: where we gather for celebrations, where my father's coffin rested before his final journey to the cemetery, where tradition says a daughter's wedding rites must begin before she is married off. A place woven with memory and meaning. It's not that my mother lacked a home, she sold the city house she had shared with my father and, with her own hard-earned money, bought a new one, a place she could truly call hers. But this village house was different. It wasn't about ownership alone; it was about belonging, connectivity, deep-rooted traditional ambiance, it was about the story of our family and the visible recognition that we were part of it.

Yet, even with homes of their own, my father's family has pulled this one too tightly in their grasp as if we don't exist, as if my father had no wife, as if we, his daughters, have no claim to the heart of his heritage. They have treated the house as though it belongs only to the sons, as though our presence there is borrowed and conditional.

After my father's death, the question of this house should have been simple. My mother was his wife, we were his children, and in any fair world, our place there would have been unquestioned, but fairness was never part of the unspoken rules in this family. Those rules were written in favor of sons and silence. My mother chose not to fight; she said it softly but firmly: "Peace is worth more than walls." She didn't want to spend her life in courtrooms or begging relatives who had already humiliated her. She had built her own home — a sanctuary no one could take — and she wanted to move forward, not live chained to old battles. I understood, but I also struggled. Part of me wanted to march into that house with papers and truth. I wanted to stand for my mother the way she had always stood for us. I wanted to say:

"This is not just any property. This is the house where my father's coffin left for the grave. This is where my sisters and I will one day stand to be married. This is heritage — and we belong to it too."

I wanted to force them to face the injustice of cutting us out while keeping the very house that symbolizes family, but another part of me knew what my mother knew: some fights cost more than they give back. She had spent years reclaiming her dignity after heartbreak and exclusion. To wrestle for this house would mean returning to the same people who denied her worth, it would mean letting them define the battlefield, and she refused to give them that power. So, I stayed silent — at least outwardly. Inside, though, I dreamed of a different ending: one where a wife didn't have to ask for keys to the home she shared with her husband, one where daughters weren't erased from the place where ancestors lived and family rituals are meant to be held, one where the men who already have homes of their own wouldn't still reach to claim this one too.

I know some would say, "Move on, it's just a house," but in all honesty, it is never just a house, it is root, it is identity, it is acknowledgment. It is the difference between being family and being tolerated. Even now, I feel the quiet fire of that injustice. It doesn't consume me, but it fuels me.

It drives me to build spaces my own children will never have to beg to enter. It reminds me why I write, why I tell our story so that silence will not win and daughters will not disappear.

My mother chose peace, and I respect that choice with all my heart, but a small part of me still hopes that one day she might change her mind, that she might decide to stand and claim what rightfully belongs to her and to us. Maybe she never will, maybe she is too tired to fight, and I cannot blame her. Yet some quiet hope remains that before all is said and done, she will choose to be seen and to take back what was always hers. For my mother, I sense that some battles we sometimes need to fight for validation are not necessary — probably when it will cost you your mental health, drain you physically, and often times, if caution is ignored, it might become a huge conflagration that might incinerate one's soul or family. I believe in my mother, I trust her judgment because over the years, her silent battles have led us to become better and stronger. I just wish we fought for what was truly ours and made our stand.

CHAPTER 15
THE SONS THEY CHOSE – AND LOST

For years, the family clung to the belief that sons would carry the name, the wealth, the honor. They poured their loyalty and resources into the boys my father had outside his marriage. They gave them keys, literally and figuratively. Doors opened for them that stayed shut for us. Surnames were signed over easily. Property rights were defended fiercely. We were told, in a thousand small ways, that they mattered more, that they were the essence of life, sons were the root, and we, daughters, were just a petal; we will eventually fall off, wither and die.

But life, in its quiet, unrelenting way, writes its own truth. The sons they chose — the ones they believed would uphold the family name — drifted down darker roads. Some fell into crime, some into drugs, some stole from those who had once defended them, and others cycled in and out of prison. Promises of greatness dissolved into court cases, police visits, and whispered shame. The very name they were given to "carry" became associated with scandal and disappointment.

But not all of the boys were strangers to me. One of them, my brother, just two or three years older, became someone I deeply loved. He had been conceived before my father met my mother, but we never knew about him. When he first came to stay with us, I felt uneasy, even angry. Angry that my father had kept him a secret from us, and especially from my mother, when she married him and built a life without knowing the whole truth. That hidden history made it hard for me to accept him at first; he felt like a living reminder of a betrayal my mother hadn't deserved.

But he turned out to be nothing like the threat I imagined. Instead, he became a friend, almost as if we shared the same mother. We were close in age, close in spirit, bound by a quiet understanding that transcended the divisions adults tried to keep. He loved my mother despite everything he had been told about her. He saw the real woman she was: kind, strong, patient, and he made up his own mind. My mother, in turn, stepped in where my father had failed him. She became present when my father was absent. She provided what he needed because he was respectful and full of love.

Watching her care for a son who was not hers by birth, a boy she had been judged for not bearing, was one of the greatest lessons of my life. She loved him simply because he was her husband's child and because he was good to us.

We grew into our teenage years almost like siblings born of the same womb. We talked about everything. I remember nursing him after his circumcision ceremony, teasing him later once he healed, and we could laugh about how he walked in those early days. I remember when our father, one of the few times, handed us his medical aid card so we could both get gold teeth; it was the trend then. He chose a full gold tooth; I got a little gold triangle.

My mom and I laughed because he couldn't stop grinning just to show it off. He even poured water into a basin and bent over, saying he could see his gold tooth's reflection. He had so much potential — an exceptional soccer player, talented, and full of life. My mother encouraged that dream and backed him every way she could. In a life full of broken promises from his own father, she gave him the love and support he deserved.

Then life struck another cruel blow: he was taken from us. Shot and killed a few years after my father's passing. His death shattered something deep inside me. It broke my mother too — the same woman who had been tormented for not having sons, yet chose to love another woman's son as if he were her own. Losing him felt like losing a piece of our fragile hope that love could rewrite old wounds.

Even now, I can picture him, his grin flashing that gold tooth, his soccer dreams alive in our yard, his easy way of loving us. His loss is a wound that never fully closes.

Meanwhile, the daughters they had written off were quietly building lives. We studied. We worked. We cared for one another. We built families and homes. We stayed out of trouble. We became women who carried dignity and strength — not because it was handed to us, but because we learned to create it in the absence of protection. We became the very legacy our father could have been proud of, if only the family had seen our worth sooner.

I remember hearing whispers about one of the other boys getting into serious legal trouble and feeling a complex knot inside me: pain for a brother I had once hoped to know, and an unshakable anger at the hypocrisy of a system that had empowered him while dismissing us. They gave him everything, ranging from the name, the house, and the approval, yet still, he was lost. We, who were denied almost everything, built something out of nothing.

It's a cruel irony, but it's also a quiet truth: worth is not decided by gender or by favoritism. Character grows where love and fairness live, and it withers where entitlement and injustice rule. I don't rejoice in their failures. I grieve the broken men they became; I grieve the brother I loved and lost; I grieve the family that might have been if love had been evenly given. But I also hold my head high because in the silence where we were dismissed, we created something beautiful. We proved — without shouting — that daughters are not a disappointment, we are strength, we are resilience, we are legacy.

Sometimes I wonder if the family sees it now, if behind closed doors they realize the cost of their choices. If they see that the sons they protected have struggled, while the daughters they pitied are standing tall, maybe they know, maybe they don't, but I no longer need their acknowledgment. The truth lives in the lives we've built and in the quiet, powerful fact that the ones they chose became lost, while the ones they cast aside became the backbone of the story.

CHAPTER 16
BREAKING THE SILENCE, OWNING MY STORY

For most of my life, silence felt safer. It was the language of survival, the silence my mother chose when doors slammed, the quiet I learned when phone calls cut me down, the quiet that kept peace even when peace cost dignity. I grew up believing that maybe if I stayed small, stayed polite, stayed unseen, the world would hurt less.

But silence also erases. It erases wives who built homes but were dismissed; it erases daughters who were celebrated at birth only to be diminished later; it erases the truth of what happened and allows others to rewrite it however they choose. I lived long enough to see my own story twisted by people who hadn't walked a single day in my shoes, and I knew, finally, that if I didn't speak, someone else would keep deciding who I was. It began quietly — a whisper inside: tell the truth. At first, I didn't imagine books or videos or public words. I only wanted my children to know the real story.

I wanted my daughters to grow up knowing their grandmother was strong, that being female is not a flaw, that silence is not the only option. I wanted my son to understand that manhood is not about erasing or dominating women, but about protecting and honoring them.

So I began to write. Some days the words came like a flood, other days they crept out slowly, shaking with the weight of old wounds. I wrote about the little girl whose father danced in the streets when she was born — before the whispers of "only girls" began. I wrote about my mother studying with babies at her feet, buying her own home when the world turned its back. I wrote about the humiliation of asking for a key to my father's house. I wrote about the brother I loved and lost. I wrote about the sons who were chosen while we were cast aside — and what life taught us all in the end.

Writing was not easy; it felt like peeling back scars. It meant reliving rejection and betrayal, naming things our culture prefers to keep hidden, but every page I finished felt like reclaiming ground.

I was no longer waiting for someone else to invite me into the story; I was taking my rightful place in it, and with every chapter, something in me shifted. I began to stand taller. My voice, once small and cautious, grew steady and resounding. The little girl who tried so hard to prove she was enough was replaced by a woman who knows she already is.

My mother's dignity lives in me, but so does a fire she could not always afford to show. She chose peace to protect us; I choose truth to honor us. Breaking the silence also became a way to heal. Pain that once felt heavy and private became purposeful when I shaped it into a story. Each word said to the world: we were here, we mattered, and you cannot erase us.

Each line gave my children, and maybe other daughters out there, permission to believe the same. I know my words will make some people uncomfortable. They may deny, defend, or dismiss, but I am no longer writing for their approval. I am writing for the little girl I was, for the women who raised me, for my children, and for anyone who has ever been told they don't belong.

Silence kept me safe once. But truth sets me free now. And as I write, I feel the ground shift — not for those who refused to see us, but for me and the ones coming after me. The story is ours again.

CHAPTER 17
CROWNED WITH GLORY

For so long, the story of my life felt like a fight just to be seen. First, as a daughter, celebrated and then quietly diminished. Then as a girl learning that her gender could cancel joy. Then, as a woman watching doors slam — keys withheld, names denied, truths rewritten. I carried pain, but I also carried my mother's dignity, my own quiet fire, and the love we built despite rejection. And somewhere along the way, without asking permission, I began to rise. It wasn't one dramatic moment. It was a thousand small, defiant steps. Going to school and excelling because my father had planted a love of language and my mother had shown me discipline.

Turning early motherhood — which some thought would end me — into a masterclass in resilience, shaped by the nights I once stayed awake caring for my baby sister. Building a home, a career, and a voice even when no one handed me a path.

It was writing.

It was teaching.

It was telling stories so children would know their worth.

It was standing in classrooms and shaping young lives, the way I wished someone had fought to shape mine.

It was crafting books and lessons and characters that honor daughters, lift mothers, and teach sons to respect.

It was living a life bigger than the limits they placed on me.

And the bitter irony still stings: for years, my mother was blamed for not producing a son — whispered about, pitied, diminished, yet science tells a different story. It's the father's chromosome that determines a baby's sex. Mothers give life; fathers decide whether that life is male or female. My mother carried the shame of something she never controlled, while my father was celebrated. Knowing this truth doesn't erase the hurt, but it exposes the injustice for what it was — ignorance dressed as culture.

Slowly, people began to notice — not always the ones who hurt me, but others. Students who see me as more than just a teacher; parents who trust me with their children; readers who find courage in my words; my own children, watching and learning that womanhood is not a cage but a force. I am no longer just the girl who was pitied for being born female. I am a woman creating a legacy. I often think of my mother when I feel this strength. She could not always fight the battles I wanted her to, but she fought for something else — survival with grace. She built a home when they tried to take hers, she raised daughters who became powerhouses, and she refused bitterness even when it would have been easier. Her peace built the foundation on which my fire now stands.

We are different kinds of warriors, but we fight for the same truth: that women matter, that daughters that love matters more than favoritism or tradition. The world once tried to write me off, to cast my mother and me into the shadows of "only girls," but here we are — standing, creating, thriving. The very ones dismissed as unworthy have become educators, storytellers, nurturers of futures, builders of homes, writers of new narratives. And so, I crown this story not with the approval of those who withheld it, but with the dignity we forged ourselves. A crown made not of gold or inheritance, but of survival, courage, love, and truth. A crown that says: We endured. We built. We reclaimed the story they tried to erase.

I know the pain will always live somewhere in me — the locked doors, the name denied, the brother lost, the unfairness. But it no longer defines me. I am more than what was taken. I am more than their silence. I am the living proof that daughters are enough.
We have turned shame into strength.

We have turned loss into legacy.

We have turned exclusion into purpose.

Crowned — not by them, but by our own resilience.

CHAPTER 18
BUILDING A LIFE BEYOND THEIR EXPECTATIONS

I look at my life now and feel something I once thought I might never feel: peace. Not because the story behind me is gentle, but because I have made something beautiful from what was meant to break me. I was the firstborn who watched joy fade when the word "daughter" was spoken too many times. I was the child who saw doors locked, names withheld, a mother shamed for something she could not control. I was the teenager who held a baby sister while studying for exams, who stayed awake to keep a home running because the world wouldn't show up for my mother. I was the young woman who loved and lost a brother, who reached out for family and was told to be silent. I was the daughter who saw her mother rebuild dignity from rubble — and learned to do the same. Every wound shaped me, but none defined me; they became tools in my hands.

Motherhood came to me not as a mystery but as a path I'd walked before. Caring for my last-born sister had taught me how to hold a baby, soothe a fever, and juggle sleepless nights.

So, when my own first child arrived and my mother asked gently if I needed help, I could smile and say, "Don't worry, Mom — I've got this." In a way, life had been preparing me all along, and with that preparation came a decision: I would raise my children differently. I would teach my son that girls are enough, more than enough. I would raise him to honor, to respect, to protect without diminishing. I would raise my daughters to know their worth so deeply that no one's silence or bias could shake them. Our home would not repeat the mistakes that scarred mine.

I have built a life of my own design, one that many once doubted I could have. I am a mother, an educator, a writer, a storyteller. I am shaping young minds in classrooms and beyond, teaching language and confidence and respect. I am writing books that honor girls, uplift mothers, and help sons learn kindness and strength. I am turning pain into purpose, silence into story.

There are still days I wish things had been different — that my father's family had chosen love over favoritism, that my brother had lived, that my mother's rightful place had been honored.

I still hope, somewhere deep down, that one day my mother will change her mind and fight for what belongs to her and to us — that she will claim the home where her husband's coffin left for the grave, where one day my sisters should stand to be married. But whether she does or not, I know now that our worth is not waiting behind anyone's permission.

I am living proof that the daughters they dismissed have become the backbone of the story. We are thriving, we are raising the next generation differently, we are breaking cycles and rewriting the narrative. They wrote us off — but we wrote our own ending. And as I close this chapter, I know my crown was never theirs to give; it was forged in long nights, quiet courage, uncelebrated victories, and relentless love.

It sits not on my head alone, but on my mother's, on my sisters', on every woman who has ever been told she is less.
We are not less.

We are legacy.

We are enough. And we are building lives beyond their expectations.

ABOUT THE AUTHOR

Thuli Marutle Leigh is a South African-born international ESL teacher and author whose storytelling blends truth, courage, and reflection.
Raised Without Worth, Crowned With Glory is a powerful and deeply personal story about the silent pain endured by women who give birth to daughters in societies that value sons more. It reveals the emotional and generational scars caused by favoritism, rejection, and cultural bias
- where a mother's worth is unfairly measured by the gender of her children.

Through raw honesty and reflection, Thuli Marutle Leigh sheds light on how these experiences shape daughters who grow up feeling unseen yet destined to rise. It is a story of healing, dignity, and divine restoration - showing that even when society strips a woman of her worth, she can still stand tall, reclaim her identity, and wear her crown with glory.

www.ingramcontent.com/pod-product-compliance
Lightning Source LLC
Chambersburg PA
CBHW030235170426
43201CB00006B/228